Parent
on
Purpose

Janis Hanson

I am dedicating this book to you ~

a dedicated parent.

Jake & Christy,
what a priviledge
to come along ride as you
parent on purpose!
Jesse

CONTENTS

TWO ARE BETTER THAN ONE

"Two are better than one, because they have a good return for their labor." Ecclesiastes 4:9 NIV

Apart from *God,* I am nothing! I am *eternally* thankful for my husband, Dave, who was the first to share with me the name, Jesus Christ. Also, the countless hours editing and contributing to the book.

I am thankful for my children~

> Ryan I love the most because he was my firstborn.
> April I love the most because she was my firstborn daughter.
> Evan I love the most because he was planned.
> Aaron I love the most because he was a surprise.
> Karina I love the most because God intervened.

I am thankful for their spouses~

> Heather because she recruited the "beta test group" (thank you to everyone who endured that group!), formatted the book, and created the cover!
> Jeremy for his technical expertise, and making us laugh.
> Ali, who diligently proofread and edited the workbook. (Coma?)
> Tessa, who is the best thing to happen to all of us.

I am thankful for my grandchildren~

> Sienna, Connor, Vivian, Adeline, Jacinda, Aria and.......
> Gramma loves you! ♥

I am thankful for my friends~

> Martha for being my biggest fan and proofreading.
> Flamingos: Marla, Carrie and Susan for adding love and laughter to my life.
> Jack and Cynthia for being an instrument of change.
> And all those who have walked beside me!

One last thank you again to my husband, who gave me the freedom to retire (thank you Renee too), and encouraged me to do one thing… *"Write a parenting book!."*

FOREWARD

Janis Hanson has written a very practical guide for parents who are looking for tools which will help them train up and nurture their children. She uses a blend of solid Biblical principles and humorous personal stories to help parents understand how these principles can be applied in the appropriate settings. Janis has hammered these principles and practices them out in the workshop of her own home.

My wife, Susan and I have known Janis and her husband Dave for over 25 years. Together we have watched our three children and the Hanson's five children grow up to be strong men and women of faith. We have cried, laughed, prayed for our kids and talked together about these principles. To her credit, Janis was nominated by her children for the "Mother of the Year Award." (She won.)

Janis has given all parents a wonderful set of helps in this workbook, which, if applied, will bring peace to the family and point children in the right direction for life. - Dr. Mark vonEhrenkrook

~~~

My husband, Steve, and I met Janis and Dave Hanson as our Sunday school teachers at Trinity Bible Church in Phoenix, AZ in 1986. Janis and I began trading babysitting time. I was unprepared for my 2nd son whose very strong temperament was already producing a battle of wills with me by age 2. He would not stay in bed and I just kept returning him over and over to his room. I shared with Janis the issue we were having, and she introduced me to "creative correction". I watched in absolute amazement as this little boy quickly changed his attitude about staying in bed!

I cannot advise you strongly enough to take these parenting principles to heart that Janis has invested her time and talents into!
- Martha Brack, RN, BSN

Janis Hanson

INTRODUCTION

*"It takes courage to make the choice to be satisfied.
It takes courage to invest the excess in others when you could be
indulging yourself. It takes courage to say no to wants that would
only complicate your life. Loving takes time and time requires
sacrifice ...somewhere. Effective parenting cannot be done by
accident. We have to parent on purpose."*

Tim Kimmel, Little House on the Freeway

That quote from Tim Kimmel inspired the title *Parent On Purpose.* The fact that you have begun this workbook makes you a brave parent to me already! I agree with Tim that effective parenting takes courage, and it is an investment of your time. And yes, you may need to make some sacrifices somewhere, however, the payoff is HUGE!!!

- What if you could just speak *one* time and your child would respond?
- What if your two year old would go to bed when you say it is time?
- What if you could lie in bed in the morning and your children would get up and get ready for school without you harassing them?
- What if the siblings resolved their own conflict? (*Uh huh, I got you now!*)
- What if your teenager would look you in the eyes and treat you with respect?

These are just some of the things I experienced and enjoyed with effective parenting. Granted, I am not saying it was like this *every* day, but it was the major part of my parenting. Please know my objective in writing this is not to put out the perfect child, but rather for *you* to not be put out as a parent. What exhausts a parent is the constant asking, telling, pleading, begging and counting in a given day, and waking up to start it all over again. That can all come to an end as you begin your journey with me.

I know it was my commitment to effective parenting that enabled me to engage in so many challenging roles, in addition to raising our five children. Initially, I started out as a Respiratory Therapist straight out of college. I had somehow managed to get a medical scholarship in my senior year of High School, even though I wasted many years partying. I continued that lifestyle into college and was struggling to maintain a 'C' average in order to keep my scholarship. In particular, I was flunking chemistry. However, in the front row of chemistry class, I spotted a tall former Marine with a pocket protector who looked like he could tutor me. Little did I know, that he would not only help me pass chemistry, but help me pass from *death into life.*

In all my growing up years I had not once heard the name Jesus Christ, (I will share more about my childhood in another chapter). It was during one of our tutoring sessions that I first heard the verse, John 3:16, "***For God so loved the world, that he gave his only begotten Son, that whosoever believeth in him should not perish, but have everlasting life."*** *KJV* When I heard that verse I heard only one thing, that I was loved! God loved *me.* I think of Cinderella, and how foolish it would have been for her to say no to the glass slipper, and stay enslaved to her wicked stepmother. I had also grown up with a wicked stepmother, and I was desperate to be loved and saved. I grabbed salvation, like it was the glass slipper, and was immediately transformed!

I ended my partying lifestyle, and began a lifetime commitment on a spiritual journey. I went from failure in school to graduating with a 4.0, and rose to the top of my field in just a couple of years. I became a Critical Care Respiratory Therapist on a transport team that picked up preemie babies in rural areas, and brought them to our state of the art hospital in Tucson. In addition, I was very involved with a discipleship ministry on campus called the Navigators. I was actually considering going on staff with them to become a girl's missionary worker, when I fell in love. Yes, I married my chemistry tutor, Dave. ☺

We went on to have five children, and while raising them moved eight times. During all my parenting years, even though I left the medical field to stay home and parent, I continued to grow and serve. I taught Bible studies, began and led a women's ministry and served in adult ministries with my husband. I volunteered in the schools, and counseled couples in marriage and parenting. I taught myself calligraphy and had a successful home business. I became the director of an abstinence program and helped write the curriculum that is still being used today. In addition, I led seminars, spoke at women's retreats and worked 20 years as motivational speaker.

I am sharing this with you to simply say, I could not have done all that if I was overwhelmed in parenting. The simple parenting principles, that I practiced diligently, freed me up to serve because I was not spent! I know that not being spent as a mom on a daily basis also helped our marriage (I am throwing this in for free! ☺).

~~~

My hope is this workbook can spare you years of frustration and grief. I ask that you patiently go through the workbook principle by principle to build a parenting model that will stand. Typically, parents are desperate to get to the latter chapters of correction and sibling rivalry, but grasping the basics in the first chapters will make those seem effortless! You will see that there is limited written work because the majority of the homework is simply applying the principles in your home. Look for this picture at the end of all the chapters for specific activities.

I have included the Bible verses in the back of the book in case you are doing this in Starbucks (I am from Seattle). However, I was limited to using the King James Version, so you may want to bring the translation that you are familiar with.

This workbook was designed with just you in mind. However, you can do it together with your spouse, with a small group of parents, or as a bible study. Having you and your spouse on the same page is always better. Networking with other committed parents is also helpful. I am just thankful that you are getting started! It is a privilege to come along side of you as we have come along side of so many. ♥ Thank you.

And may you say with conviction, when you are finished… *"Please raise my children for me!"* Just kidding! My sincere desire for you is that you love parenting as I have!

CHAPTER 1

Laying the Foundation

1st PARENTING PRINCIPLE

Love your children the way God loves us.

While living in Tucson, Dave and I were just one of the many couples fortunate enough to be mentored in a marriage study by a godly couple named Jack and Cynthia Heald. Cynthia went on to write a series of books; *Becoming a Woman of Excellence, Prayer,* etc. But she could have written the book on parenting!

We began watching how Jack and Cynthia parented their four children, who were a complete joy to be around. Contrast that with our firstborn son, Ryan, who was out of control. I was adamant about not disciplining our son like I had been disciplined, but I had little direction for what it should look like. Today I can hear Dr. Phil say, *"And how is that working for you?"* Ryan was throwing fits in Target, emptying cabinets at friend's homes and refusing to hold my hand crossing busy streets. I finally conceded that I did not have a clue how to parent!!! We humbled ourselves and asked for help, and that encounter changed the course of our lives!

The foundational principle that Jack and Cynthia taught us was, *to love our children the way God loves us.* Below I have some examples from the Bible of how God loves us and how we can apply it to our parenting.

God as our Heavenly Father:

1. Romans 8:35

    a. How does God love *us* in this verse?

b. How can this be applied to parenting?

_____

_____

God's love is unconditional! This kind of love was not demonstrated in my own home where I watched my parents become alienated from my siblings for a variety of reasons. That alienation fostered hostility among the siblings, and a sense of insecurity for me.

> (Not) *"I love you because......*
> (Not) *I love you if..............*
> *I love you period!"*
> *Marge Caldwell*
> (Parentheses mine.)

"We love because He first loved us." I John 4:19 NIV

2. Psalm 103:8-13

a. How does God love *us* in this passage?

_____

b. How can this be applied to parenting?

_____

_____

God's love wants nothing to come between us. When the children were very young we illustrated how sin can separate us from God, and each other, by using ©Legos. We built a wall and showed how it can separate using 'action figures' on each side. Each brick of the wall represented unresolved conflict which can lead to feelings of resentment and bitterness. Then we dismantled it and said, *"Tearing the wall down is like saying you are sorry and forgiving each other. We do not want even ONE brick standing between any of you!"*

Our children had plenty of conflict, but for the most part, we were not involved. (I will share more in the sibling rivalry chapter). However, we stayed on the scene until there was *no brick standing.* Now that our adult children are married, we often hear how thankful their spouses are for this character trait we have instilled. Also, my favorite byproduct of this is the strong and loving relationships all five of our children have with each other.

3. Proverbs 5:21-23

    a. How does God love *us* in this verse?

    b. How can this be applied to parenting?

Dave and I were more committed to our children's character than their privacy. We had an open door policy. They could shut the door, but at ANYTIME we could enter. *"Not on my watch"* was something I often said to my adolescent and teenage children.

4. John 17:9

    a. How does God love *us* in this verse?

_____

    b. How can this be applied to parenting?

_____

_____

Many times our children would leave the house and the reality that I have no control over what happens to them would make me anxious. I became convicted that if I had time to worry then I had time to pray.

> *"Prayer goes where you cannot follow."*
> *Jill Briscoe*

5. Hebrew 12:10,11

    a. How does God love *us* in this verse?

_____

    b. How can this be applied to parenting?

_____

_____

Verse 11 in the Amplified Bible elaborates the fruit that comes with discipline.

"A harvest of fruit which consists in righteousness -- in conformity to God's will in purpose, thought, and action, resulting in right living and right standing with God."

That is the fruit we are hoping for as we *parent on purpose*; the fruit of right standing before God. What a shame it would be, if in the end, your children did the right thing for the wrong reason. Without a change of heart or conviction, they would do what is right in your home, but out of your sight abandon those same convictions.

Read Mark 6:30-52

Write down everything Jesus did, and what He asked the disciples to do?

_____

_____

_____

_____

_____

_____

Write verse 52 in your own words.

_____

_____

_____

The disciples did what they were told to do but missed the truth about who Jesus was. They did not have a change of heart or belief. Are there any guarantees that the investment I am asking you to make will bring about permanent change in your child; change that would result in doing the right thing for the right reason? No, it is not 100%. However, there are several studies including the International Bible Society and The Barna Research Group, that indicate 83% of people who come to Christ do so between the ages of 4 and 14. This is when you have them!

"Love the LORD your God with all your heart and with all your soul and with all your strength. These commandments that I give you today are to be on your hearts. Impress them on your children. Talk about them when you sit at home and when you walk along the road, when you lie down and when you get up."
Deuteronomy 6:5-7 NIV

You simply live a life of loving God and share that life with your children on a daily basis. Jesus demonstrated this with His disciples. He reinforced the truth by modeling, teaching, telling stories, praying, spending time with them, and so on.

~~~

Here are just a few of the things I did on a regular basis to reinforce the truth with my children:

- In the morning when they were all ready for school, I read fun character building books. This also served as a great motivational tool to get ready on time as they could hardly wait to read the next chapter.

- I had a special snack waiting on the table after school. This would encourage them to stop and gave me a chance to ask questions about their day. Most of my questions were geared to the *unstructured* time in their day like recess and relationships. Some of our most meaningful talks were at this time because it was fresh in their mind.

- Driving them to and from events I would make up stories, usually about "Lucy Ladybug", that had moral dilemmas and solutions. I would involve them in the solutions so they had to be good listeners. The added benefit was my sanity with peace and quiet in the car! ☺ I also had *Odyssey* tapes from *Focus on the Family* that reinforced the truth when I needed a break.

- Most evenings we tucked them into bed with a brief scripture-based book or the Bible, relative to their age, and prayed. My husband read the entire *Chronicles of Narnia* series to our boys twice!

(One of my favorite children's books was, *Big Thoughts for Little People, by Kenneth Taylor,* who also wrote the *Living Bible.* I loved the illustrations. Each page had an alphabet theme and taught Biblical character. In addition, you had to find the hidden ladybugs, which started the whole ladybug theme in my stories! I am also crazy about Glen Keane's Adam Raccoon series. Pretty impressive that Glen is a directing animator for Walt Disney Pictures.)

Of course this is not an exhaustive list of passages of how God loves us, but you can see where I am going. The bottom line is that *before* you respond to your child, stop and remember how God responds to you. All of our principles will rest on this foundational truth. How can we possibly go wrong attempting to love our children the way God loves us?

~~~

This foundational principle of loving our children the way God loves us, may seem daunting. After all, God is perfect and we are not! However, with the gift of salvation, we were transplanted in Christ and placed in the best of soil. That soil came with ©Miracle Grow already in it! Have you ever read the back of the box of ©Miracle Grow and all that it promises?

❖ Helps Prevent transplant shock.

❖ Promotes strong vigorous growth.

❖ With regular use flowers can thrive in the hottest days.

❖ Rich in iron and essential nutrients for flowers that are suffering.

❖ Engineered to disperse just the right amount.

That miracle grow is the Holy Spirit given to us at salvation. We have everything we need to respond godly as parents. We can thrive in the worst of days!

In fact, I heard a speaker once say that instead of saying I *have* the fruits of the Spirit; say I *am* the fruits of the Spirit! Swapping that one little word inspired me to write this:

With your Spirit I soar
            over mountains and valleys; rivers of tears.
                  I am joy, I am peace,
                        I can overcome fears.
I am love.
            Forgiving is easy to be;
                  having all goodness
                        because of your Spirit in me.
And with your Spirit I wait,
            with patience all mine,
                  no reason for bitterness
                        being filled I am kind.
How glad I am
            that to self I have died.
                  Such a life I now have
                        with Your Spirit inside!

In your home this week ask yourself, *"How does God love me?"*, before responding to your child.

Janis Hanson

CHAPTER 2

Parenting Style

2nd PARENTING PRINCIPLE

Make it a goal to be a loving and firm parent.

It will be helpful to identify your *initial* parenting style as we begin the workbook. Gary Smalley's book, *The Key to Your Child's Heart,* suggests the following four styles:

1. Dominant
2. Neglectful
3. Permissive
4. Loving and Firm

How would you define these styles? *(Dictionary / Thesaurus)*

Dominant:

_____

_____

_____

Neglectful:

_____

_____

_____

Permissive:

_____

_____

_____

Loving and Firm:

_____

_____

_____

Write the corresponding parenting style to the comments below.

"I am going to count to
three." _____

"Get your mother to help
you." _____

"I need more information before I can make a
decision." _____

"Rules are rules! No child of mine is going
to…" _____

What do you remember hearing from your own parents?

_____

_____

_____

What parenting style did your parents demonstrate?

Mother: _____

Father: _____

(The style your parents demonstrated is your first point

of reference.)

What do you think you are communicating as a parent?

_____

_____

_____

What is your parenting style? (Think through each child.)

_____

What does your spouse say is your parenting style? (Just sayin... ☺)

_____

I think you would agree with me that we all want to be loving and firm parents. ♥ The rest of the workbook will take you deeper and deeper into how to become a loving and firm parent. But first, let's address what prevents us from being loving and firm parents.

There are many obstacles to becoming loving and firm parents. Some possible obstacles could be fatigue with both parents employed outside the home, distractions with the vast technology, and the ability to bring work home. Another one could simply be a lack of parenting tools.

A huge diversion in our parenting today is the internet. We invest an exorbitant amount of time in taking care of business, communication, and even recreation online. The other day I was babysitting my two year old granddaughter, Vivian, and we were playing restaurant. It was my turn to be the waitress and when I approached her she said, _"Wait a minute."_, as she pressed imaginary buttons on her imaginary cell-phone.

She is learning young!

I can also relate to not having the necessary tools in parenting. I always tell people I have a *Cinderella story*. My mother died when I was just months old and this drastically changed the dynamics of our family. My dad became a neglectful father with four little girls under the age of six. He married, what I perceived to be, the wicked step-mother, who brought two sons of her own. They went on to have two more children, and in short order, we became a dysfunctional family of 10!

My stepmother was a dominant parent, while my dad was neglectful. I cannot remember a single time when the physical contact from either parent was tender. What parenting style do you think I demonstrated with my first child? My natural inclination was to love my child, but to NOT be firm. In the absence of knowing what to do, I did nothing, and started out as a permissive parent.

~~~

Given your background, or the many obstacles, making it a goal to be a loving and firm parent may seem impossible. Let me introduce a tool that could help. My husband has a ratcheting screw driver that he got 34 years ago. Regardless of the fact that it has been replaced ten times over with technology, and is now held together with duct tape, it remains his favorite tool. *"It's simple and it works!"* he says.

One of my favorite tools in life is a concept called *goal vs. desire*. It's my 'ratcheting screw driver'. I got this tool 30 years ago when I read the book, *The Marriage Builder,* by *Larry Crabb.* This is my go-to tool in my marriage, friendships and parenting. It's simple and it works!

Goal vs. Desire:

A *goal* is something that you want that does not involve another person (or any factor beyond your control). You own it 100%.

A *desire* is something that you want that does involve another person.

Let's have a little quiz.

Is it a *goal* or a *desire* that you have a good marriage? _____

You cannot make it a goal to have a good marriage because that involves your husband. A good marriage can only be a desire, but you can make it a goal to be the best wife/husband you know how to be.

At the time I am writing this Dave and I have been married 34 years. But sadly, I spent too many of those years discontented trying to make what could only be a desire into a goal. Hopefully, you will be using this tool early in your relationship, and focus more on what you are able to control and pray for what you do not.

Is it a *goal* or a *desire* that you lose weight? _____

You own this 100%; making it a goal. YEAH! I know you want to say to your husband… *"You made me eat that Blizzard!"* But no one puts food into your mouth.

Is it a *goal* or a *desire* that you have well behaved children? _____

It's a fantasy! ☺ Ok, a desire, and while it is an immense desire that our children behave and turn out to be amazing adults, we cannot make this a goal. Even God, who is the consummate loving and firm parent, had rebellious and unpredictable children.

> *"I reared children and brought them up," God says in Isaiah 1:2, "but they have rebelled against Me." NIV*

What should the goal be in parenting?

I can remember vividly the day Dave and I decided to make it a goal to be loving and firm parents! We had been counseled by Jack and Cynthia and we were ready to go home and apply the truths we learned. Being consistent and effective was hard on all three of us! Thankfully, after that difficult transition, we began enjoying the role of parenting, and not surprisingly were invited back to friend's homes again. ☺

In your home this week listen to how you talk. Do you sound like a loving and firm parent?

CHAPTER 3

Instruct

3rd PARENTING PRINCIPLE

Give instructions for the purpose of teaching
or to deter disobedience, disrespect
and irresponsibility.

We never have to *teach* our child to be selfish or instruct them to stop sharing too much. All of us are born with a self-seeking, greedy, crooked, sin nature. Children start out early with *'MINE!'* and *'ME'*. They are predisposed to grabbing toys from siblings or friends, pushing to be first in line, and screaming when they want something.

> *"Foolishness is bound up in the heart of a child."*
> *Proverbs 22:15a NASB*

Being fully aware of this truth made me an unwavering parent. Instructing a child is vital to restoring him or her to all that is good and right.

> *"God turns man's value system upside down. 'What is highly valued among men is detestable in God's sight.' Luke 16:15 Man cares about externals, but God cares about inner qualities. Man values beauty, brains, wealth, and power; God values a pure heart. Integrity and faithfulness have greater value to God than success."*
> *Jean Fleming, A Mother's Heart*

Are you committed to what God is committed to in the area of restoration? To answer that simply look at where you have invested your time and resources as parents. Has it been mainly on education, sports, appearance or technology? Parents often make intentional, consistent investments in their child's college fund, but little investment in their child's character.

"Some people treat life like a slot machine,
trying to put *in as little as possible and hoping to hit a jackpot.*
Wiser people think of life as a solid investment from which
they receive in terms of what they put in."
Roger Hull, Reader's Digest

I am asking you, as a parent, to invest in a three-step restoration process.

Restoration Process:

1. Instruct
2. Reflect
3. Correct

Over the course of these next few chapters I will explain at length how to carry out each step. I guarantee a huge return on your investment! The first step, instruct, takes a considerable amount of time initially, but it is the key to the restoration process. It will also help meet the objective of you not being spent as a parent.

There are four reasons why you stop and instruct:

1. Teaching
2. Disrespect
3. Disobedience
4. Irresponsibility

Define each of these words, and in the latter three, give an example of how a child might display them.

Teaching:

_____

_____

Disobedience:

_____

_____

_____

_____

Irresponsibility:

_____

_____

_____

_____

Disrespect:

_____

_____

_____

_____

Teaching is explaining to a child the right behavior. You will see many examples of this all throughout the workbook. Wrong behavior comes in the form of disobedience, irresponsibility and disrespect. Disobedience is failure to follow instruction. Most parents are quick to recognize and act on disobedience. Irresponsibility is simply childish, immature behavior, such as fooling around the table and knocking the milk over. Disrespect can come in many forms such as rolling of the eyes, stomping the feet and not making eye contact. Parents often underestimate the long-term consequences of irresponsibility and/or disrespect. We are stopping to instruct for *all three* behaviors. If we ignore any one of these, there is a ripple effect, like a rock in a pond. For example, if you allow your child to be disrespectful to you by stomping their feet, this child could go on to be rude to a sibling, talk back to a teacher, disregard the law, or walk away from resolving marital conflict. This could be far-reaching.

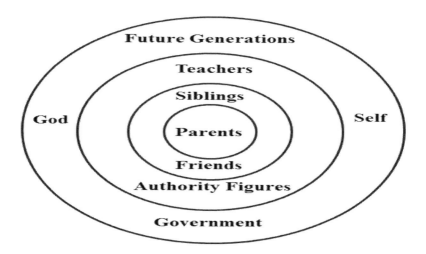

For this reason, I am adamant about not letting ANYTHING go!

What behavior is your child doing that is driving you crazy right now?

Check one or more of the reasons below that corresponds with the behavior you identified:

__ Disrespect

__ Disobedience

__ Irresponsibility

What do you want from your instructions?

__ Change of attitude

__ Specific behavior

__ A task performed

You have identified the reason you need to give your child instructions and what you want your child to do. But before you speak, I want you to think exactly what and how you will say it to best motivate the child.

Ten Tips for Instruction:

1. Instruct at eye level.

"Look at mommy."

You are face to face with the child and making eye contact with each other.
Making eye contact shows that you mean business and forces the child to focus on you. I would reinforce this skill

by playing a game. As long as the child maintained eye contact, I would give them an M&M every 30 seconds or so. If they break eye contact, that ends the game.

Teaching your child to make eye-contact is a life-long skill. You will thank me, in the future, when your teenager makes eye contact with you and other adults. This may need to be your very *first* instruction.

"Sweetheart, let's play a game. Mommy has four M&M's. What colors are they? You get to have all of these if you look at my eyes as I talk to you, and I will look at you! Keep looking at mommy's eyes while I talk and you will get all four! Here is your first one. Keep looking. Wow! Good job the next color is yellow, etc."

If the child looks away while you are talking, that ends the game and they lose the remaining candy. Return to the game in short order to teach the skill for good!

2. Speak with a kind but firm voice.

"Sweetheart, I see you picked Grandma's flower from her garden. These flowers are here for us to just look at."

3. Keep the instructions as positive as possible.

"Let's keep our hands to our sides as we walk around and look at the flowers. Come smell this one? Wow!

Children respond better to positive instruction instead of *"Don't touch the flowers."* This also reduces arguments.

4. Use age-appropriate instructions.

A small child may need to be distracted from the garden, where an older child can receive instruction. When in doubt, network with other parents, and use the infinite resources online for what instructions are age-appropriate.

5. Clarify the instructions by having your child repeat them back to you.

"What did mommy say about Grandma's flowers? Yes, you get to look at and smell the flowers. Show mommy how you do that? Yes, good job keeping your hands to your side."

You can also role-play the desired behavior.

6. Give an older child the opportunity to be a part of the decision making.

"Sweetheart, look at grandma's beautiful garden! What should we do when we are playing out here?"

An example of this was when I wanted my daughter to wear a dress. I gave her the option of three dresses from which she could pick. This moved us beyond the argument of, *"Do I have to wear a dress?"*

Involving the child also teaches decision-making, and helps meet the objective of you being less spent as a parent.

7. Be sensitive to factors such as illness, fatigue, etc.

In some instances you may need to take into account factors that contribute to a child not responding, and limit or eliminate instructions. Some of these factors may be missing naps, changing the schedule, etc.

8. *"Talk less; say more." Swedish Proverb*

Let your instructions be short and concise.

9. **Pick your battles carefully.**

A familiar phrase but worth repeating! You need to follow-through on *every* instruction, so let the little infractions go such as mood swings, childish play, etc.

> *"Hardness of your child's heart is always a battle that you cannot ignore. Do not be overly focused on the details of a given infraction; rather, focus on your child's heart."*
> **USS Parenting / Navigating the Seas of Modern-Day Parenting**

10. **Share what the child has to gain/lose.**

While you are giving instructions even a small child will weigh their options. *"What will I gain if I obey? What will I lose if I don't'?"* Therefore, this should be addressed in almost all of your instructions to highly motivate the child to respond correctly.

In the garden example, the child gains the fun of walking around the garden, looking and smelling the flowers. They will also gain praise from doing what is right. Never underestimate the power of a parent's praise. However, if the garden is too tempting for our self-indulging little terror ☺, then he/she may take the risk of plucking with little to lose. I am thinking it all out before I ever speak to the child, and considering what will motivate this child to do what is right?

Let's put all of our ten tips together for our final instruction. We want this child to *respect* property. We want a *specific behavior* of not wreaking havoc in grandma's garden.

"Sweetheart, look at mommy. You can walk around Grandma's garden with your hands to your side, looking at all the flowers. They are so pretty and you can smell them too! We also have water toys to play with. But if you step on/touch/pull grandma's flowers, I will shut off the water and you will have to come in the house. Tell mommy what you will do in Grandma's garden now. Good!"

Good instructions take practice, and perhaps brainstorming with other committed parents, but keep in mind the pay-off. No more frustration, counting or screaming. You simply shut off the water immediately when your child touches a plant in the garden. The next time you are in grandma's garden the child knows exactly how to behave.

*I will be sharing more options of what a child may *lose* when I cover correction in chapter 4.

Using the 10 tips, write instructions for the following examples:

You want your child to sit still at the dinner table.

_____

_____

_____

_____

_____

_____

You want your child to stay in bed.

_____

_____

_____

_____

_____

_____

You are now ready to write good instructions for the behavior that is driving you crazy (page 30).

_____

_____

_____

_____

_____

_____

Did you consider what your child would _gain/lose_ with your instructions?

What will they _gain?_ _____

What will they _lose?_____

Here are a couple more examples of instructions I have given to my children:

1. Ryan's Rules for Roaming

We were renting a home where the play yard was in the *front* of the house. It was not the greatest situation, but I needed Ryan to play only in the yard and not venture out on the sidewalk or street.

"Ryan, honey, let's bring some toys out to the yard. Wow, they are going to be so fun to play with. Ryan, look at mommy, I am going to walk you around this big space and show you everywhere you can play. Every place that has grass you can play. Does the sidewalk over here have grass? No. Does the street have grass? No. Do you play on those? No. Tell mommy now where you can play with your toys? If you step on the sidewalk, or any place that does not have grass, mommy will bring you and your toys in the house. Tell mommy what will happen if you step on the street.

Mommy is going to always be out here with you, and we are going to have sooo much fun!"

2. How Clean is Clean?

A few times a year I wanted the children to clean their rooms thoroughly. Not assuming they knew what this meant, I had the older children create a list of things they thought they should do, and helped the younger children write their list. This helped with 'buy in'. I praised them for their ideas and added a few of my own. I helped the younger children clean their rooms, but to motivate the older children to work independently, this is what I said:

"In an hour mommy is going to come in your room. I will go over the list with you and if everything is done I will give you $2.00! (That was a lot back then). *For every item not completed on the list, I will take a quarter away, and you will not be paid until it is all done according to what we agreed."*

With the instructions in writing and agreed upon, I knew they had understood. What will they *gain/lose?* Of course they gain and lose the monetary award. They gain my praise, and a clean room which they love to play in. In addition, peer pressure helps here too. After the hour was up and the children paid, it was interesting to hear the dialogue between them about how much they got paid, and what they will do different next time.

In the future, I simply said, *"Let's get the lists and do a good cleaning",* and they were off and running. No begging, screaming, counting, etc. How nice is that!

~~~

I hope you are excited about giving good instructions. This is where you can have the greatest impact on shaping a small child's character into the image of what God desires. God has given you this role and I sincerely hope you have the courage to do it.

"Ortho," means to make straight, upright or correct and "paideia" is child; child rearing. When God chose you to parent, He also chose to partner with you in His 'state of the art' Orthopedic Institute. He has a lot of employees, *parents,* and a comprehensive network of services such as the *Bible, Holy Spirit, prayer, fellow believers, etc.*

He is committed to the restoration of individuals, and has employed your services to straighten out the children He has given you. You are vital to His plan and you have limited time.

"Our children are not our prized possession to do with what we want, but are simply passing through our lives on to theirs."
Howard Hendricks

In your home this week stop and give good instructions. Please try and keep your calendar as clear as possible so that you are giving effective instructions and able to follow through.

CHAPTER 4

Reflect

4th PARENTING PRINCIPLE

Reflect before you correct.

"The most important step in building character is to establish reasonable expectations and boundaries in advance. Children should know what is and is not acceptable behavior before they are held responsible for those rules. This precondition will eliminate the overwhelming sense of injustice that children feel when they are punished for their accidents, mistakes and blunders. If you haven't defined it......don't enforce it!" James Dobson

I agree with Dr. Dobson. Before correcting a child, we need to be absolutely certain it is warranted. For this reason, we are going to stop and *reflect* before we correct. But first, I want to go back to the foundational truth of parenting the way God parents us, and have you look at some passages that affirm the restoration process that I am asking you to invest in.

Read Genesis 2:15-17 and Genesis 3:1- 2. What did God want from His instructions?

    __Change of attitude
    __Specific behavior
    __A task performed

Thinking about the ten tips for instructions, which ones did God demonstrate with His children, Adam and Eve?

_____

_____

_____

What would Adam and Eve *gain* if they obeyed God's instructions?

_____

_____   _____

What would Adam and Eve *lose* if they did not obey?

_____

_____

Read Genesis 3:18-23 and write your observations about God's parenting?

_____

_____

_____

_____

Here are some of my own observations regarding these passages:

- God made sure that His children understood His instructions.
- In Genesis 3:11 God asks them, *"Have you eaten from the tree that I commanded you not to eat from?"* God already knew what they had done but He appealed to their conscience.
- And again in verse 13, *"What is this you have done?"* God holds them accountable.
- Notice how God's correction was both immediate and related to the offense. We will come back to this principle in the correction chapter.

All throughout the Old Testament we see how God stops to give instruction, and follows through with correction. Let's look at a couple more passages as we continue to observe the perfect parent model.

> **Read I Samuel 15:1-3 and record God's instructions to Saul.**

_____

_____

_____

> **What was Saul's response in I Samuel 15: 7-9?**

_____

_____

_____

> **What was God's response in I Samuel 15: 10-11?**

_____

_____

_____

I Samuel 15: 13-21 is the classic response we get as parents. The children deny it all, argue with us, and blame someone else! I can hear myself say over the years of parenting, *"STOP!"*, as I can relate to Samuel in verse 16.

I love the verses that speak to what God is committed to as a parent in verses 22 and 23.

Paraphrase I Samuel 15: 22-23 in your own words:

_____

_____

God does not let even a *little* disobedience go! We are going to attempt this, as best we can. Your children should know that every time you speak, you mean what you say! However, God is God and we are not. We, as parents, are not infallible and may need to take time to *reflect* before we correct. Even God, as the perfect parent, reflected on rare occasions.

> **Look at II Kings 22:16-20 and record what God's response was to the contrite heart of Josiah?**

_____

_____

_____

God saw the softened heart of Josiah and reconsidered His plan of action. Below are a few questions to ask as you reflect and consider the next course of action.

Questions to reflect on:

1. Am I certain they heard and understood my instructions?

An example of this could be a parent flippantly saying, *"Clean up."* What do those words *really* mean to a small child? Begin with a clean slate and assume the child knows nothing. You may need to demonstrate, or role-play, the desired behavior or task.

Here is an example of role-playing, "clean-up":

"Let's play with your blocks together!" After playing with your child say, *"Look at mommy now. We are going to play a game* (always a good way to motivate a small child) *when I say the words, 'please clean up', you quickly put all the blocks back, and put the bin back where we got it from. What are the words I will say? Tell mommy what you will do when I say those words. But wait until I say the words. I am going to go way over to the other side of the room. Wait for those words.*

'Please clean-up!' Wow, look how fast you are going! Do I see any blocks around? Is the bin back where it belongs? Good job!"

Remember the last tip with our instructions? What will they *gain/lose?* When you set it up as a game the child is motivated literally by 'winning or losing' the game! Later when you ask your child to please clean up, and they defiantly say no or walk away, you can move with certainty to the third step of correction.

Another example of this, was when I was a young mother trying to get out the door with all five children. If I had to beg, chase, scream, and count to ten in order to leave the house, I would be exhausted before I even left the driveway. Instead, I role played the words, *"time to leave"*, when I did <u>not</u> have to go anywhere. The game was to see how quickly we could put our shoes and coats on, climb into car seats and buckle up, when I said the words, *"Time to leave."*

After role-playing the expected behavior a number of times, they knew exactly what I meant when I said it was time to go. I remember family and friends marveling at how easy it was for us to manage all five kids, and I was thinking, "It definitely was *not easy*, but it had paid off."

In addition, as our children matured, we did some written contracts for dating, times to be home, etc. Our teens could never say, *"You didn't say that."*, because we had written it down and agreed upon it.

2. Were my instructions wise?

In this case, you may have been too quick to speak or overreacted. It happens. (I am sure my kids could give you examples☺). For instance, telling a child he cannot play video games for a week for an infraction may be difficult to follow-through with, and may add more stress to the situation.

> *"Be absolutely sure that your children are capable of delivering what you require. Impossible demands put children in an unresolvable conflict. There is no way out."*
> *James Dobson*

If this is the case, you simply need to humble yourself, and say, *"I spoke too soon; let mommy think about this."*

3. Are they mirroring my behavior?

If you have been flippantly telling your children what to do, and rarely following through with anything, it is all falling on deaf ears. You can hardly correct a child when you have been inconsistent. With erratic correction there is a sense of injustice on behalf of the child. I would simply say, *"Mommy has been letting this go, but I am on it now."*

I can remember our oldest daughter, April, treating her siblings with disrespect, which was out of character for her. She was answering them with curt and rude remarks. I was intent on correcting her, until I stopped and listened and heard my own voice mirrored back as I had been short-tempered that week.

Rather than correct April, I had to go back to all the children and ask for forgiveness for my attitude.

"Model the rules; teach the rules; enforce the rules."
Ron Rose

This is not an exhaustive list of possible questions to ask as you *reflect* on the situation, but it is a good start. With good *instructions* you seldom need to make any changes. However, when you are certain *correction* is warranted you may move to the next step with conviction and courage!

 How are you doing in the following?

- Are you watching for disrespect, irresponsibility and disobedience?
- Are you stopping to instruct?
- Are you thinking through what they will *gain/lose*?
- Are your children responding to your voice the *first* time you speak?
- Are you following through *every* time?
- Are you seeing change?

I am sooooo proud of you! ♥

Janis Hanson

CHAPTER 5

Correct

5th PARENTING PRINCIPLE

Follow through with correction.

As a society, we have tuned out God's voice and lost our moral footing. Without any direction in values, or teaching right from wrong, children are left to their own demise and are free falling. The German proverb, *"The apple does not fall far from the tree."*, suggests the obvious. We are seeing the absence of good parenting come into fruition.

In contrast, let's see the fruit of effective parenting with a mother I have admired from the past. Susannah Wesley was the youngest of twenty-five children! She was born in 1669 to the family of Dr. Samuel Annesley, a well-known powerful minister. She went on to have 19 children of her own in 19 years! She is best known for her two sons, John and Charles Wesley, who would impact generations to come for the Gospel of Christ. Charles wrote hundreds of hymns such as: *And Can It Be That I Should Gain, Christ the Lord Is Risen Today, and Hark! The Herald Angels Sing.*

Biographer Arnold Dallimore notes: *"Susanna trained her children to obey and in so doing richly molded their characters."* She never disciplined excessively or unkindly. She would schedule a private time with each child once a week to develop personal and spiritual growth. When Susannah was asked by her adult son to write down her tips on parenting, this is what she said about correction: *"For by neglecting timely correction, they will contract a stubbornness and obstinacy which is hardly ever after conquered and never without using such severity as would be painful as to me as to the children."*

Paraphrase Susannah's quote regarding correction.

_____

_____

_____

Dave and I are passionate about investing our time teaching parents of *small* children because we, like Susannah, have seen the difficult challenge of turning a teen around. I also appreciate Susannah sharing that correction pains *her* more than the child. Once again, it reminds us of the verse in Hebrews, *"All discipline for the moment seems not to be joyful, but sorrowful; yet to those who have been trained by it, afterwards it yields the peaceful fruit of righteousness." Hebrews 12:11 NASB*

What are your initial thoughts about disciplining a child?

_____

_____

_____

What did you appreciate about how you were disciplined?

_____

_____

_____

What did you *not* appreciate?

_____

_____

_____

I shared with you earlier about my permissive parenting as a result of my harsh upbringing, and not wanting to discipline my first born son, Ryan. What I *did* appreciate about how I was raised was that I was punished for my misdeeds. I believe the fear of being punished kept me reigned in, somewhat, as a lost teen. What I did *not* appreciate was that I was always punished but never corrected.

I want you to think about the difference between punishment and correction. I typically will use the word correct vs. discipline because in our culture today discipline has become a negative word, and perhaps correction would be better received. And in truth, the word correction, or **yaw-kahh'**, is used more frequently than the word discipline in the Bible.

Punishment vs. Correction:

Purpose of punishment:

_____

_____

_____

Purpose of correction:

_____

_____

_____

Attitude of the parent punishing:

_____

Attitude of the parent correcting:

_____

Child's response to being punished:

_____

Child's response to being corrected:

_____

Punishment penalizes the child for their past misdeeds. It creates frustration and hostility on the part of the parent, and fear and guilt on the part of the child. On the other hand, the purpose of *correction* is to train and correct future behavior. It is motivated by love, and concern for the character of the child, and promotes a feeling of security.

I am going to share seven steps of *correction* which may, at first glance, appear tedious. But trust me when I say it gets easier for you as a parent, and becomes a royal pain to the child, which is exactly what we want! And I promise correction will decrease over time as you *parent on purpose.*

> *"Every year that passes should bring fewer rules, less direct discipline and more independence for the child." James Dobson*

A few random thoughts before we begin:

- James Dobson suggests a possible age of 15 months to begin correction.
- Remember, for the very small child praise and distraction may be enough to encourage the right behavior.
- Diligence in the privacy of your home will reduce correction in public. YEAH!
- Correction <u>always</u> follows good instruction and reflection.

OK here we go! Let's get ready to R....U....M....B....L....E!!!

Seven Steps of Correction:

1. Isolate your child.

This avoids any embarrassment or "saving face" on the part of the child. It also allows time for reflection for both parent and child. For example, I would simply say, *"Meet me in the bathroom"*. This would give me a few minutes to calm down, and possibly reflect or think through a course of action. In addition, the child would have time to hopefully soften his/her heart (OR NOT).

Designate a neutral location. What location might work for you? It could possibly be the utility room, pantry or laundry room. For our examples I am going to be using the laundry room.

My husband liked the bathroom because he had a place to sit down! ☺

2. Ask your child, "What did you do?"

This directly appeals to the conscience of the child as God demonstrated in Genesis. We want to appeal to their God-given conscience.

> *"For this is the covenant that I will make with the house of Israel after those days, saith the Lord; I will put my laws into their mind, and write them in their hearts."*
> *Hebrews 8:10. KJV*

We want to avoid any manipulative statements that could create an emotional, argumentative or volatile response.

Match each of the manipulative statements below with one of the four options listed.

- Intellect
- Will
- Physical
- Emotional

"You will have to be punished for what you did!"

_____

"You hurt me when you did that."

_____

"Promise me that you will never do that again!"

_____

"Did you think that was a smart thing to do?"

_____

We talked earlier about reinforcing the truth so that our children do the right thing for the right reason. Here is a good opportunity for you to use this as a teachable moment. The question needs to be, *"What was the right thing to do before God?"* Our desire is to help develop in our children a sensitivity to the Spirit of God.

"There is a sort of sensitiveness in his soul which makes him discern between good and evil. When God the Holy Spirit is dealing with him, there is a true, enlightened conscience within him, so that he no longer puts bitter for sweet and sweet for bitter, or darkness for light and light for darkness; but something within him tells him, "This is right," or, "That is wrong." It is a most blessed thing when this is the case, and it is always the work of the Spirit of God."   *C. H. Spurgeon*

3. Communicate love and parental commitment.

For example, *"I am not going to let anything go because I love you, and that love wants the best for you!"*

What other words could you use to communicate love and commitment?

_____

_____

_____

4. Carry out the correction.

(In Chapter 2, I said I would share some *correction* options. Below are some possible ideas that you could include in your *instructions*.)

a. Verbal Correction

Always use the *least* amount of correction. A firm *verbal* correction may be all you need to change the behavior/attitude of a small child. How will you know if it was effective? The behavior is NOT repeated. However, the verbal correction is not done flippantly. You are still using all seven steps with this form of correction.

"Connor, meet me in the laundry room. What did you do? Yes, you hit your sister. Was that the right thing to do? No. What should you do now? Yes, we need to go to sissy. Thank you for telling mommy so nicely. Give mommy a hug; mommy loves you sooo much! Let's go out and ask sissy to forgive you for hitting her."

In addition, I remind the child that I will, "up the ante", with a repeated offense. *(gain/lose)* I may not have it all figured out at the time, but I want the child to know that it will definitely be more severe. (Hopefully, just the thought of going back in the laundry room will deter the behavior and you will never need to figure it out! ☺)

"Connor, if you hit your sister again, we will be back in the laundry room immediately. And this time mommy will have to think of something more to correct you with. Tell mommy what will happen if you hit your sister again?"

b. Physical Correction

The Bible is quite clear regarding the use of physical correction.

"Foolishness is bound in the heart of a child; but the rod of correction shall drive it far from him." Proverbs 22:15 KJV

"The rod and reproof give wisdom: but a child left to himself bringeth his mother to shame." Proverbs 29:15 KJV

"He that spares his rod hates his son: but he that loves him chastens him early." Proverbs 13:24 KJ 2000 Bible

When choosing this option, consider using a neutral object rather than your hand. Often, I would simply place a wooden spoon on the counter to remind the children that I am on it, and that was enough to deter them. Remember, the least amount of correction to change the behavior.

Please be aware of what your current state law allows, especially if you have your child in a public institution.

For example, I live in WA State and searched under *correcting a child* and found our WA policy:

RCW 9A.16.100 Use of force on children-Policy-Actions presumed unreasonable.

It is the policy of this state to protect children from assault and abuse and to encourage parents, teachers, and their authorized agents to use methods of correction and restraint of children that are not dangerous to the children. However, the physical discipline of a child is not unlawful when it is reasonable and moderate and is inflicted by a parent, teacher, or guardian for purposes of restraining or correcting the child. Any use of force on a child by any other person is unlawful unless it is reasonable and moderate and is authorized in advance by the child's parent or guardian for purposes of restraining or correcting the child.

The following actions are presumed unreasonable when used to correct or restrain a child: (1) Throwing, kicking, burning, or cutting a child; (2) striking a child with a closed fist; (3) shaking a child under age three; (4) interfering with a child's breathing; (5) threatening a child with a deadly weapon; or (6) doing any other act that is likely to cause and which does cause bodily harm greater than transient pain or minor temporary marks.

The age, size, and condition of the child and the location of the injury shall be considered when determining whether the bodily harm is reasonable or moderate. This list is illustrative of unreasonable actions and is not intended to be exclusive.

I am a mother not a lawyer, but to me this law is well balanced. It recognizes the need for parents to correct children while protecting children from abuse.

"Do keep in mind that someone with good intentions may have differing opinions on what classifies as abuse and are mandated to report any concerns."
Ali Hanson, Elementary Teacher, MA in Teaching

It was always my intention to know, and keep open communication, with my children's teachers. I am very aware of the changing culture and hope that you as a mother are staying as informed as possible.

c. Creative Correction

Being creative means you are attempting to relate the correction to the offense. For example, if your child is hitting others you might say, *"Keep your hands to yourself or I will give you a chore in the house where you can use your hands to help and not hurt."*

The creative correction could be a reward system. *"Mommy wants you to do what is right and be kind to others. I am going to put 4 quarters in your jar. If you keep your hands to yourself today, I will give you another quarter to put in your bank. But for every time you use your hands to hurt, you will give mommy a quarter. At the end of the week, let's see how many quarters you have and we can go shopping as a reward!"*

Remember to keep the creative correction simple because you will need to follow through with *whatever* you set up. I do not want to add stress to your day with a complicated sticker system. As an alternative, consider using what I call, "computer currency". A child can *earn* or *lose* computer or video game time in their "bank". This could control the time the child plays, and it would be extremely motivating.

Also, you can involve the child in the process. *"Mommy needs to correct this behavior/attitude. What correction do you think we should use? You can pick it this time, but if you do it again Mommy will pick."(gain/lose)* I was always surprised to see how firm they were with themselves.

Use your creative genius, and if you are 'found wanting', network with other committed parents. On occasion, I have told my children, *"I am going to correct you for this but let me think about what I am going to do."*

Practice *creative* correction for the following and try to relate it to the offense.

Your child is pinching his/her sibling.

_____

_____

_____

Your child does not sit still at the dinner table.

_____

_____

_____

Your child does not stay in bed.

_____

_____

_____

The goal is to have the correction be <u>immediate and over!</u> This is where I separate from the pack of professionals. I seldom used time out, and not once did I use grounding. In our relationship with our Heavenly Father, there is never a moment in time that we do not have access to Him. It is comforting to know that He does not alienate Himself from us. ♥ Time-out and grounding separates you emotionally and physically from that child/teen.

Dragging the correction out with, **"Go to your room!"**, may actually add to your stress. In all reality, the child may not be developmentally able to process what you had intended, and is simply left to play and forget. On the surface it may appear like a quick remedy, but with little cost to the child, the unwanted behavior/attitude is often repeated. In the long run, this will wear you down as a parent. We don't want you spent! More importantly, very little is accomplished in the area of restoration, resolving the conflict, or improving the character of the child. Lastly, there will be less chance of your child harboring animosity because you are seen as a fair and just parent. As far as it is up to us, we want to maintain a right relationship with our children as they grow into adulthood.

5. Watch for a tender heart.

You are looking for signs that the child is sincerely sorry. Evidence of a softening heart could be quietly crying. There may need to be instruction given to the child that this is *always* the expected outcome when being corrected. There is no tolerance for screaming, kicking or tantrums (from the child ☺). You should be able to hug or kiss your child when the correction is over. And if not, we start the process all over again *(gain/lose). I hope I am not overwhelming you!*

6. Establish your child's responsibility.

The child must go back, *always and immediately,* to make it right. Instruct them to speak kindly and make eye contact with the offended party and say, *"Do you forgive me for_____? (the offense)."*

Only the courageous and committed few go here. I seldom see this done, but it is necessary for a couple of reasons. It is important for your child to strive to maintain a clear conscience with others.

> **"So I strive always to keep my conscience clear before God and Man." Acts 24:16 NIV**

Second, it resolves conflict with the offended party. (I will be sharing in a later chapter how this paid off in big dividends with my adult children.)

If they are unable to make it right as you instructed, it is back to the laundry room (*gain/lose)*!

7. Self-Evaluation.

It is not over yet. Quickly process how the *correction* went.

- *How did that go?*
- *Did the child have a soft heart towards me?*
- *Did my child make it right?*
- *How was my attitude?*
- *Did I overcorrect?* And if so, I will go and make it right immediately with that child.

This may all seem tedious, but as soon as your child understands your level of commitment, you will begin to see results. Your child will stop the offensive behavior/attitude because you are relentless! (My daughter in-law, Ali, shared with me the lyrics from a song titled, Relentless, by Hillsong United. *"You carry us when the world gives way. You cover us with your endless grace. Your love is relentless."* How sweet are those words.)

God's love is relentless and we are loving our children as He loves us. I know this is going to be difficult to implement for a lot of you, and perhaps harder on the children. I always tell the parents, when they begin to correct, to brief the children that, *"We are changing."*

 In your home this week:

- Look for opportunities to teach or role play a desired task or behavior.
- Watch for *any* disobedience, disrespect or irresponsibility.
- Stop and give good instructions.
- Pick your space for correction and begin practicing the seven steps. (I have printed the seven steps for you in the back if it helps to post it.)

The next chapter is sibling rivalry, and if you don't love me already…you will!!

CHAPTER 6

Sibling Rivalry

6th PARENTING PRINCIPLE

Teach siblings to treat each other with
kindness and respect.

❖ **1st baby** - You begin wearing maternity clothes as soon as the doctor confirms your pregnancy!
2nd baby - You wear your regular clothes as long as possible.
3rd baby - Your regular clothes ARE your maternity clothes!

❖ **1st baby** - The first time you go out on a date you call the sitter 10 times!
2nd baby - Just before you walk out the door you remember to leave a number.
3rd baby - You tell the sitter to call only if she sees blood.

❖ **1st baby** - You spend countless hours just gazing at your baby.
2nd baby - You spend a little time watching to make sure the older child is not beating up on the baby.
3rd baby - You spend a little time hiding from the children!

   Adapted from the February 1998 issue of Parenting.

I hope that made you smile, because if you have multiple children, you may not have smiled for a while. This is truly the area that can cause the greatest frustration and despair. Parents come to us asking for help with sibling rivalry more than any other parenting issue. May this chapter bring you great encouragement and free you up as a parent!

Before I add the last piece, sibling rivalry, let's do a quick recap.

- We laid the foundational truth of *loving our children the way God loves us* as seen in the Bible.

- We then began to build our parenting principles on that strong foundation. The first principle was to *make it a goal to be a loving and firm parent.*

- Next, we formed the restoration process; *instruct, reflect* and *correct.* I know this took a considerable amount of time and labor.

- Sibling rivalry simply rests now on our well-constructed parenting model.

In other words, there is nothing big to add, just a few finishing touches with some behavior modifications.

~~~

"The sibling relationship has been largely devalued in our culture, but people are slowly beginning to realize what a deep source of support their siblings can be throughout life. They share your longest, oldest connection. Nobody else has your history."
Between Brothers and Sister, Elaine Mazlish

Dave and I did not set out to have a large family. Growing up with seven siblings, where pandemonium was an understatement, I was biased. Dave had just one sister, and was mute on the issue.

After our first two children, Ryan and April, we were very thankful and content. After all, we were seen as the perfect family, having a boy and a girl. But I was exposed to a few godly families, and for the first time saw the potential for great joy. I had a new vision of what a larger family could look like, and began longing for another child.

We had to seek medical help to conceive our third child, Evan. We were still seen as the ideal family. Friends and family considered it a great blessing that we could have one last child. Without medical intervention, we had assumed we were done with our family. So we were shocked, when after three years we got pregnant with our 4th child Aaron. Now we were perceived as irresponsible parents, and often I had to take a defensive posture. I was surprised by our fourth child but definitely not saddened.

Dave and I made a date on the calendar to get him "fixed". I remember a snide remark someone made at the time, *"Doesn't look like you are broken!"* On the way to the appointment our car broke down, and that is why we have Karina! Okay, not in the car, but soon after, we conceived the last of our five children! We were then seen by the mainstream public as lunatics! But to me it has been only joy. I cannot imagine investing my life in anything more significant. I understand the value of siblings! Each child brings the potential of more support, more love and more laughter.

~~~

However, I am all too aware of the potential for grief. Siblings, and the competition that ensues, can wear even the best parent down! Realistically, in a household where there is no sibling rivalry there is no interaction. And where there is no interaction there is little potential for meaningful long-term relationships.

"Be assured that teasing, quarreling and angry outbursts between brothers and sisters happen in virtually every family. The only siblings who seem to get along all the time are those who aren't really engaged with one another."

Keys to Preparing and Caring for Your Second Child,
Meg Zweilback, RN

We want our children engaged and we can expect a certain amount of conflict with that. Our desire is not the absence of conflict, but resolving conflict with little to NO intervention from us!

With siblings you are still using the restoration Process:

1. Instruct
2. Reflect
3. Correct

What do I want from my *instruction?*

✓ *Change of attitude*
✓ *Specific behavior*
o A task performed

We want any attitude or behavior that fosters meaningful long-term relationships.

List three behaviors or attitudes you would like to see demonstrated among siblings?

1. _____
2. _____
3. _____

Overall, we want the children to treat each other with kindness and respect. But, again, what does that look like to a small child?

"Relationships are complex and words like, "share" and "be kind", while meaningful to us as adults, may not be clear to a child. For this reason, it is often helpful to role model and role play the desired behavior."

Dave Hanson♥

Let me illustrate some desired behaviors/attitudes that we believe are important and how we taught them to our children. Naturally, these are significant even with one child, but it becomes more important when the siblings begin to interact. And once again, this is not an exhaustive list.

Desired behaviors/attitudes:

1. Honesty:

You can sit down with a very small child and teach the principle of truth vs. lie by placing five pennies on a table and asking, *"How many pennies do I have?"*

"One, two, three, four, five." the child says.

"That is true. I have five pennies." Take away two pennies and state again, *"I have five pennies."*

"Noooo!" the child argues, *"You have three pennies!"*

"That is the truth! I have three pennies. Saying I have five pennies would be a lie. We want to tell the truth! Mommy will ALWAYS and IMMEDIATELY correct you for lying!"

Place a number of pennies before the child and ask the child to tell the truth and a lie with how many pennies there are, making certain the child caught the desired behavior of honesty. After the teaching time the pennies go in the child's piggy bank.

2. Sharing:

Sit down with a *new* toy between you and your child. You play as a parent with the toy first, being animated so as to keep the child's attention. The desired behavior while your child waits is quietly being patient. You may need to instruct the child that this is appropriate and expected behavior while waiting. After a few minutes, give the toy to the child and say, *"Your turn now! I am sharing."*

After the child plays with the toy for a few minutes say, *"My turn please."* You can elaborate if you see your child hesitate, which is their natural bent. *"Please share with Mommy, and I will give it right back to you after I play with it. But if you do not share I will have to put it away"(gain/lose).* If the child does not give it back quickly, put the toy out of sight. Come back the next day and do it all over again. Once you see the child understands the concept of sharing and waiting nicely, praise the child and give the toy as a reward!

3. Listening and communicating:

"We are going to play a game!" Again I am using my go-to motivational tool. Using a small stuffed animal or a ball, explain, *"In this game you do not want to be holding the ball. To pass the ball you have to ask someone a question that cannot be answered with a no/yes. For example, 'What did you do at recess?', would be a good question. But, 'Did you go out to recess today?', they could say, no/yes. I am holding the ball so I will ask*

the first question. I do NOT want to have the ball."

Ask the first open-ended question, and hand the ball to that person who answers, encouraging them to ask the next question.

In addition, to reinforce this behavior, when we had someone over for dinner, family or friends, I would often sit with our young children and help them write open-ended questions for our guests. They could hardly wait till their question was pulled. This taught our children to not only be good communicators, but to be good listeners as well. To this day, I love watching our adult children hang out with one another. They are all good friends who communicate on an intimate and caring level. This is not caught, it's taught! Pun intended. ☺

4. Resolving Conflict:

"The sounds of kids fighting can make even the most easy-going parent long for the serenity of a padded cell."
12 Ways to Tame Sibling Rivalry, Kathy Henderson

One of the most important behaviors we want to instill with siblings is the ability to resolve interpersonal conflict, *on their own!* (Heads up; this is going to be loooooong.)

"Children, come sit down and look at me. Today we are going to learn how to be kind and play nicely together. This is sooo important that I have a surprise for you when I am done!"

The parent gives *one* of the children a toy; for our example let's use a fire engine, and I will name the two children after two of my grandchildren who are siblings, Sienna and Connor.

"Connor, what do you do if you want to play with the fire engine? Do you grab it away from Sienna like this?" Role- model grabbing. *"Do you pull Sienna's hair? Do you scream and shout? Noooo. You play with something else or you ask nicely, 'please may I have a turn?' Let's practice asking nicely now."*

Have them share back and forth by asking nicely. Instruct them that this is the only acceptable behavior and you will correct them in the laundry room for anything else.

~~~

"Let's give the fire engine back to Sienna now. This time, Connor, let's pretend you do not ask nicely and you grab the fire engine away from Sienna. What should Sienna do?"

Give the children time to come up with their own solution.

"Does Sienna grab it back like this? Does she pull your hair? Does she scream and shout? Noooo. She should ask nicely, 'Please give that back.' And Connor, what should you do right away when Sienna asks nicely? YES!!! Give it back soooo fast. When you are playing, I am listening to see if you are being kind! The child that is not being kind I will bring to the laundry room."

Children need to know that you are their advocate if they do the right thing! The side benefit of this is tattling will decrease to the point of elimination. Each child knows the behavior I expect of them. The outcome is predictable, if they do the right thing I am on their side, and if they respond incorrectly they will always suffer the consequences. Correct immediately the guilty party with the seven steps of correction.

I realize that this will require ALL of your attention after you implement it but it is critical to saving your sanity. Let nothing go. You cannot role-model the desired behavior too much. You may be living in the laundry room for the first few days, but I promise big dividends with this one!

What will they gain if they follow these instructions?

_____

What will they lose?

_____

But we are not quite done with conflict resolution...

"Let's practice this again. It's almost time to give you the surprise! Connor, what if Sienna is jumping on your back and you want her to stop? What do you do?"

Give the child time to respond. The answer you should get immediately is, _"Please stop"._

"Do you shove Sienna off in a mean way? Do you scream and shout? Nooo! You ask nicely, 'Please stop'. What should Sienna do right away? What if you ask her nicely and she does not stop? You come to mommy and I will take Sienna to the laundry room. Remember, you cannot come to mommy until you ask her to stop~ nicely! But you will not need to come to mommy. Sienna will stop when you ask nicely, because she does not want to stop playing and get corrected. You were such good listeners!!! Here is your surprise for listening so well.

Mommy is going to be watching how you play, and I want to hear those kind words, 'Please stop' or 'Please may I have that?'. I want you to have fun playing together, and not have either one of you leave to be corrected."

Okay, now we are done! Phew, that was long but I hope it was helpful.

Take two of the attitudes or behaviors that you listed above, *(a long time ago ☺)*, and come up with a creative way to teach them to a small child.

    1. Attitude/behavior:_____

    _____

    _____

    _____

    _____

    2. Attitude/behavior:_____

    _____

    _____

    _____

    _____

Let's see how you do with some additional scenarios:

    1. Connor hits Sienna and Sienna hits back. What should be done?

    _____

    _____

"It doesn't matter what anybody else does, you do the right thing."
(I cannot even begin to guess how many times I said this to
my children growing up! I am sure they will barf when they
read it!) Both children did the wrong thing and need to be
corrected.

2. Sienna shares with you that Connor hit her and she
asked him to stop. Connor denies it all! What do you do
as a parent?

_____

_____

My input on this one is to confront them both making eye
contact.

*"Tell me the truth. The truth is ONE story and not two! I am
going to put you both in the laundry room and when I come back
in, I want the truth."*

This accomplishes a few things. First, they usually end up
with one story because they know I will go to the end to
resolve everything, ALWAYS. The conflict between them
typically ends in the laundry room when they end up
agreeing on a resolution. Also, they both know that the
correction is SEVERE for lying and this highly motivates
them to tell the truth. Peer pressure helps!

If, however, they do not come up with one story in a short
amount of time (be thankful this is extremely rare ☺), the
parent will have to judge as fairly as possible. Everyone has
a tic when they lie, and it will be in your best interest to
discover it. Also, everyone has a history helping you to
judge accordingly. Trust yourself, you know your children.

"Mommy gave you plenty of time to tell the truth. You still have two stories. One of you is still lying. God has given me the role of being fair, and I am committed to your character."

I decide who I believe is the guilty party, based on tics and history, to remain in the laundry room, and I correct them in private.

Once again, I ask the parents when dealing with sibling rivalry, to be relentless the first week. You will need the emotional and physical stamina to follow-through with the instructions. The end result is that you will intervene less often, and not be worn out as a parent. I have often said, listening to my children resolve their own issues is like background music. ♥

~~~

As you can see, Dave and I invested a great deal of time instructing our children how to treat each other. Remember I said there are big dividends with this one?

- Initially we saw it impact the younger siblings as they imitated the right behavior of their big brother or sister. That brought harmony and peace to our home.

- It continued with them being and choosing wise friends and making a difference in their community as leaders.

- It played out again in the work place, as we saw our adult children serve with integrity and a spirit of excellence in their chosen fields.

- We continue to see it in their marriage relationships as they are quick to resolve conflict.

- And finally, we watch them raise our beloved grandchildren with the same expectations, and on and on it goes.

I have been intrigued for years how one generation affects another. Parenting can change the course of history! (No pressure ☺ .)

 In your home this week:

- Role play any desired behaviors that you want to implement.
- You may need to start over if you have older children who have been mistreating each other for some time. Debrief them and say, "*We are changing how we treat each other.*"
- Be observant and in the background.
- Be brave and consistent.

Janis Hanson

FINAL THOUGHT

7th PARENTING PRINCIPLE

Make a commitment to parent on purpose.

I sincerely hope I have helped you. Do you remember the objective of my writing the workbook?

_____

_____

Are you feeling more in control and less spent? Are you experiencing more joy in parenting?

I loved my role as a mother! I loved helping to shape a small child into what God intended. I even enjoyed the teen years. I miss it all! I can remember it like it was yesterday, Dave and I sitting in lawn chairs watching the five children play together, and me sharing that I wanted to freeze time right then. I did not want it to end. I believed that what I was doing, parenting the five children God had given me, was paramount. All the time that I had invested in parenting had been worth it.

In closing, let me share one last parenting principle with you. Kay Coles James wrote an article called, *That Delicate Balance.* She was the Secretary of Health and Human Resources for the commonwealth of Virginia in 1994. She went from the poverty of her past to the corridors of the White House. She says this, *"Although the life God has blessed me is wonderful, it is often difficult, and sometimes I become weary to the point of tears. Most of all, I struggle to fulfill my commitment to my family."*

She went on to share that she feels like an imperfect juggler with too many balls up in the air. Some of the balls she referred to as rubber, where if they fell to the floor they would bounce.

Those might be her civic obligations, volunteer work, social life, etc. But other balls she considered crystal. If she allowed them to drop they would shatter. The balls that she considered crystal were her faith, her relationships with her husband, and raising her children.

I am asking you to sacrifice some balls that are rubber to keep the crystal one of parenting from shattering. Your children are crystal!

What other balls in your life would you consider crystal?

_____

_____

_____

What balls in your life would you consider rubber?

_____

_____

_____

Please remember that you are partnering with Your Heavenly Father in maintaining that delicate balance. May God continue to bless you in your role as you *parent on purpose.* ♥

Janis Hanson

1st PARENTING PRINCIPLE

Love your children the way God loves us.

2nd PARENTING PRINCIPLE

Make it a goal to be a loving and firm parent.

3rd PARENTING PRINCIPLE

Give instructions for the purpose of teaching
or to deter disobedience, disrespect and irresponsibility.

4th PARENTING PRINCIPLE

Reflect before you correct.

5th PARENTING PRINCIPLE

Follow through with correction.

6th PARENTING PRINCIPLE

Teach siblings to treat each other with kindness
and respect.

7th PARENTING PRINCIPLE

Make a commitment to parent on purpose.

Janis Hanson

SEVEN STEPS OF CORRECTION

1. Isolate your child.

2. Ask your child, "What did you do?"

3. Communicate love and parental commitment.

4. Carry out the correction. (Verbal, Physical or Creative)

5. Watch for a tender heart.

6. Establish your child's responsibility.
   (Do you forgive me for_____?)

7. Self-Evaluation.

Janis Hanson

BIBLE VERSES

Chapter 1 Laying The Foundation:

Romans 8:35

[35] Who shall separate us from the love of Christ? shall tribulation, or distress, or persecution, or famine, or nakedness, or peril, or sword?

Psalm 103:8-13

[8] The LORD is merciful and gracious, slow to anger, and plenteous in mercy.
[9] He will not always chide: neither will he keep his anger for ever.
[10] He hath not dealt with us after our sins; nor rewarded us according to our iniquities.
[11] For as the heaven is high above the earth, so great is his mercy toward them that fear him.
[12] As far as the east is from the west, so far hath he removed our transgressions from us.
[13] Like as a father pitieth his children, so the LORD pitieth them that fear him.

Proverbs 5:21-23

[21] For the ways of man are before the eyes of the LORD, and he pondereth all his goings.
[22] His own iniquities shall take the wicked himself, and he shall be holden with the cords of his sins.
[23] He shall die without instruction; and in the greatness of his folly he shall go astray.

John 17:9

[9] I pray for them: I pray not for the world, but for them which thou hast given me; for they are thine.

Hebrews 12:10,11

[10] For they verily for a few days chastened us after their own pleasure; but he for our profit, that we might be partakers of his holiness.
[11] Now no chastening for the present seemeth to be joyous, but grievous: nevertheless afterward it yieldeth the peaceable fruit of righteousness unto them which are exercised thereby.

Mark 6:30-52

[30] And the apostles gathered themselves together unto Jesus, and told him all things, both what they had done, and what they had taught.
[31] And he said unto them, Come ye yourselves apart into a desert place, and rest a while: for there were many coming and going, and they had no leisure so much as to eat.
[32] And they departed into a desert place by ship privately.
[33] And the people saw them departing, and many knew him, and ran afoot thither out of all cities, and outwent them, and came together unto him.
[34] And Jesus, when he came out, saw much people, and was moved with compassion toward them, because they were as sheep not having a shepherd: and he began to teach them many things.
[35] And when the day was now far spent, his disciples came unto him, and said, This is a desert place, and now the time is far passed:
[36] Send them away, that they may go into the country round about, and into the villages, and buy themselves bread: for they have nothing to eat.
[37] He answered and said unto them, Give ye them to eat. And they say unto him, Shall we go and buy two hundred pennyworth of bread, and give them to eat?
[38] He saith unto them, How many loaves have ye? go and see. And when they knew, they say, Five, and two fishes.
[39] And he commanded them to make all sit down by companies upon the green grass.
[40] And they sat down in ranks, by hundreds, and by fifties.

[41] And when he had taken the five loaves and the two fishes, he looked up to heaven, and blessed, and brake the loaves, and gave them to his disciples to set before them; and the two fishes divided he among them all.

[42] And they did all eat, and were filled.

[43] And they took up twelve baskets full of the fragments, and of the fishes.

[44] And they that did eat of the loaves were about five thousand men.

[45] And straightway he constrained his disciples to get into the ship, and to go to the other side before unto Bethsaida, while he sent away the people.

[46] And when he had sent them away, he departed into a mountain to pray.

[47] And when even was come, the ship was in the midst of the sea, and he alone on the land.

[48] And he saw them toiling in rowing; for the wind was contrary unto them: and about the fourth watch of the night he cometh unto them, walking upon the sea, and would have passed by them.

[49] But when they saw him walking upon the sea, they supposed it had been a spirit, and cried out:

[50] For they all saw him, and were troubled. And immediately he talked with them, and saith unto them, Be of good cheer: it is I; be not afraid.

[51] And he went up unto them into the ship; and the wind ceased: and they were sore amazed in themselves beyond measure, and wondered.

[52] For they considered not the miracle of the loaves: for their heart was hardened.

Chapter 4 Reflect:

Genesis 2:15-17

[15] And the LORD God took the man, and put him into the garden of Eden to dress it and to keep it.

[16] And the LORD God commanded the man, saying, Of every tree

of the garden thou mayest freely eat:

[17] But of the tree of the knowledge of good and evil, thou shalt not eat of it: for in the day that thou eatest thereof thou shalt surely die.

Genesis 3:1-2

[1] Now the serpent was more subtil than any beast of the field which the LORD God had made. And he said unto the woman, Yea, hath God said, Ye shall not eat of every tree of the garden?

[2] And the woman said unto the serpent, We may eat of the fruit of the trees of the garden.

Genesis 3:8-23

[8] And they heard the voice of the LORD God walking in the garden in the cool of the day: and Adam and his wife hid themselves from the presence of the LORD God amongst the trees of the garden.

[9] And the LORD God called unto Adam, and said unto him, Where art thou?

[10] And he said, I heard thy voice in the garden, and I was afraid, because I was naked; and I hid myself.

[11] And he said, Who told thee that thou wast naked? Hast thou eaten of the tree, whereof I commanded thee that thou shouldest not eat?

[12] And the man said, The woman whom thou gavest to be with me, she gave me of the tree, and I did eat.

[13] And the LORD God said unto the woman, What is this that thou hast done? And the woman said, The serpent beguiled me, and I did eat.

[14] And the LORD God said unto the serpent, Because thou hast done this, thou art cursed above all cattle, and above every beast of the field; upon thy belly shalt thou go, and dust shalt thou eat all the days of thy life:

[15] And I will put enmity between thee and the woman, and between thy seed and her seed; it shall bruise thy head, and thou shalt bruise his heel.

[16] Unto the woman he said, I will greatly multiply thy sorrow and

thy conception; in sorrow thou shalt bring forth children; and thy desire shall be to thy husband, and he shall rule over thee.

[17] And unto Adam he said, Because thou hast hearkened unto the voice of thy wife, and hast eaten of the tree, of which I commanded thee, saying, Thou shalt not eat of it: cursed is the ground for thy sake; in sorrow shalt thou eat of it all the days of thy life;

[18] Thorns also and thistles shall it bring forth to thee; and thou shalt eat the herb of the field;

[19] In the sweat of thy face shalt thou eat bread, till thou return unto the ground; for out of it wast thou taken: for dust thou art, and unto dust shalt thou return.

[20] And Adam called his wife's name Eve; because she was the mother of all living.

[21] Unto Adam also and to his wife did the LORD God make coats of skins, and clothed them.

[22] And the LORD God said, Behold, the man is become as one of us, to know good and evil: and now, lest he put forth his hand, and take also of the tree of life, and eat, and live for ever:

[23] Therefore the LORD God sent him forth from the garden of Eden, to till the ground from whence he was taken.

I Samuel 15: 1-3

[1] Samuel also said unto Saul, The LORD sent me to anoint thee to be king over his people, over Israel: now therefore hearken thou unto the voice of the words of the LORD.

[2] Thus saith the LORD of hosts, I remember that which Amalek did to Israel, how he laid wait for him in the way, when he came up from Egypt.

[3] Now go and smite Amalek, and utterly destroy all that they have, and spare them not; but slay both man and woman, infant and suckling, ox and sheep, camel and ass.

I Samuel 15:7-9

[7] And Saul smote the Amalekites from Havilah until thou comest to Shur, that is over against Egypt.

[8] And he took Agag the king of the Amalekites alive, and utterly destroyed all the people with the edge of the sword.

[9] But Saul and the people spared Agag, and the best of the sheep, and of the oxen, and of the fatlings, and the lambs, and all that was good, and would not utterly destroy them: but every thing that was vile and refuse, that they destroyed utterly.

I Samuel 15:10-11

[10] Then came the word of the LORD unto Samuel, saying,

[11] It repenteth me that I have set up Saul to be king: for he is turned back from following me, and hath not performed my commandments. And it grieved Samuel; and he cried unto the LORD all night.

I Samuel 15:13-21

[13] And Samuel came to Saul: and Saul said unto him, Blessed be thou of the LORD: I have performed the commandment of the LORD.

[14] And Samuel said, What meaneth then this bleating of the sheep in mine ears, and the lowing of the oxen which I hear?

[15] And Saul said, They have brought them from the Amalekites: for the people spared the best of the sheep and of the oxen, to sacrifice unto the LORD thy God; and the rest we have utterly destroyed.

[16] Then Samuel said unto Saul, Stay, and I will tell thee what the LORD hath said to me this night. And he said unto him, Say on.

[17] And Samuel said, When thou wast little in thine own sight, wast thou not made the head of the tribes of Israel, and the LORD anointed thee king over Israel?

[18] And the LORD sent thee on a journey, and said, Go and utterly destroy the sinners the Amalekites, and fight against them until they be consumed.

[19] Wherefore then didst thou not obey the voice of the LORD, but

didst fly upon the spoil, and didst evil in the sight of the LORD?
[20] And Saul said unto Samuel, Yea, I have obeyed the voice of the
LORD, and have gone the way which the LORD sent me, and have
brought Agag the king of Amalek, and have utterly destroyed the
Amalekites.
[21] But the people took of the spoil, sheep and oxen, the chief of the
things which should have been utterly destroyed, to sacrifice unto the
LORD thy God in Gilgal.

I Samuel 15:22-23

[22] And Samuel said, Hath the LORD as great delight in burnt
offerings and sacrifices, as in obeying the voice of the LORD?
Behold, to obey is better than sacrifice, and to hearken than the fat of
rams.
[23] For rebellion is as the sin of witchcraft, and stubbornness is as
iniquity and idolatry. Because thou hast rejected the word of the
LORD, he hath also rejected thee from being king.

II Kings 22:16-20

[16] Thus saith the LORD, Behold, I will bring evil upon this place,
and upon the inhabitants thereof, even all the words of the book
which the king of Judah hath read:
[17] Because they have forsaken me, and have burned incense unto
other gods, that they might provoke me to anger with all the works of
their hands; therefore my wrath shall be kindled against this place,
and shall not be quenched.
[18] But to the king of Judah which sent you to inquire of the LORD,
thus shall ye say to him, Thus saith the LORD God of Israel, As
touching the words which thou hast heard;
[19] Because thine heart was tender, and thou hast humbled thyself
before the LORD, when thou heardest what I spake against this
place, and against the inhabitants thereof, that they should become a
desolation and a curse, and hast rent thy clothes, and wept before me;
I also have heard thee, saith the LORD.
[20] Behold therefore, I will gather thee unto thy fathers, and thou
shalt be gathered into thy grave in peace; and thine eyes shall not see

all the evil which I will bring upon this place. And they brought the king word again.

All the verses are from The King James Version (Authorized)

ABOUT THE AUTHOR

Hi, thank you for your interest. I currently live in Puyallup, WA with my husband, Dave, my long haired Chihuahua Trixie, and our worthless cat. I live within a few miles of three of my adult children and their families and am very involved. Yes, that is a nice way of saying I babysit A LOT. Dave and I are serving in children's ministry at Lighthouse Christian Center, and I am enjoying retirement, writing and speaking.

Please know that I am here for you. You can send any questions or feedback regarding the book to my business Facebook page: *Parent on Purpose.*

Also, please become a follower of my blog as it is written to encourage, inspire and minister to you on a weekly basis. http://popwithjanis.wordpress.com

Janis Hanson

Made in the USA
San Bernardino, CA
07 November 2013